The Isle of Man

A POSTCARD TOUR

VOLUME THREE – THE SOUTH

compiled by

Steven Dearden and Ken Hassell

Stenlake Publishing 1997

First published in the United Kingdom, 1997,
by Stenlake Publishing
Telephone / Fax: 01290 551122

ISBN 1 872074 95 2

INTRODUCTION

This is the third volume in our series on the Isle of Man and covers Castletown and the south of the Island in the years between 1900 and 1945. All the cards illustrated once again come from our two collections and draws on the work of a number of photographers who were based in the south. Most outstanding of these was V.L. Swales who in the first half of the century chronicled all the major events in the area and produced superb photographs of the fishing industry such as the one below.

At the turn of the century the southern part of the Isle of Man was beginning to assert a significant contribution to the Island's economy. Although Douglas was the focal point for tourism, Port Erin was the main attraction in the south and the holiday accommodation that is still there today was set up at that time. Meanwhile, Port St Mary was competing with Peel's status as the main fishing port and for a time the tonnage of fish brought in actually exceeded that of the western port. Even though it had relinquished the position to Douglas thirty years earlier, Castletown still considered itself the capital of Mann and the proud community was busy re-inventing the town as a high-class tourist resort. As an 1897 Official Guide to the Island states,

> The most striking peculiarity of Castletown is its intense respectability – a characteristic which for long kept it back from joining in the modern industry of the Island, the Summer Season. It is now beginning to recognise its mistake, and is doing its utmost to fit itself to be a modern holiday resort of the better and quieter class. Its accommodation is good, its tariffs are moderate, and its surroundings are such as should make it a favourite resting-place with the better class of tourists.

However, away from the towns and villages the rural south continued with the farming and fishing industries which had supported it for generations.

Steven Dearden and Ken Hassell.

An early view of the harbour before the construction of the swing footbridge in 1903. The ketch is the *Isabella Dodd* (CT51), built in 1886 and skippered by Jack Cringle before being sold to Lerwick in 1893. The other numbered boat is the nickey *Ceres* (CT42), owned and captained by John Harrison and eventually broken up in 1923.

The lifeboat station by Castle Rushen prison, *c.*1890. The station was established in 1856 and stayed there until a new prison was opened in Douglas in 1891. Thereafter, all the nineteenth century buildings that had sprung up around the castle were demolished under the direction of Lord Raglan and the lifeboat was rehoused at the outer harbour.

The shipbuilders at Castletown and Port St Mary tended to be members of the Qualtrough family and their timber yard at Castletown occupied part of Cooil and Qualtrough's original site. The Upper Harbour, known as the 'Duck Pond' or Claddagh, was where the Castletown fishing boats and a few from Port St Mary were laid up for the winter.

The original Castletown brewery was established in 1780 on The Parade as one of the many business ventures of the Quayles of Bridge House, although it wasn't until the late nineteenth century that the new premises were opened on the quay. Under the ownership of the Cain family the brewery won first prize at the 1936 London Brewery Exhibition, an achievement of which they were obviously proud.

A bit of old Castletown, little changed from this 1935 photograph.

The funeral of Sir James Gell, Clerk of the Rolls, who was one of the most eminent and popular Manxmen of his time. He was a lifelong supporter of St Mary's church where, appropriately enough, he died in his pew in 1905.

This vessel is the *Ben Jee* of the Ramsey Steamship Company. Built in 1919, the *Ben Jee* was worked by the company from 1924 to 1933 when she was sold to the United Molasses Co.

Castletown's best known fleet of sailing ships belonged to the Karran family. They owned eleven ships over the years, the *Imberhorne* being the largest at over 2000 tons. This is the *Manx King*, built in 1884, which sailed all over the world with various cargoes, in particular nitrate for fertiliser which was shipped from South America – the clipper had to double the 'Horn' on every voyage.

On the right of this view is Bridge House which housed the first Manx bank, Quayle's Bank. It opened in 1802 at a time when the smuggling trade – previously the mainstay of the Manx economy – was being suppressed and business interests on the Island were developing in more legitimate channels. The bank was in business for eighteen years.

THE PIER, CASTLETOWN, I. O. M.

Castletown harbour was established surprisingly late. The first stone breakwater was only built in 1844-45. It had to be extended by 30 yards in 1849 and at the same time a light was erected on the seaward end which was visible eight miles out to sea.

After the new prison was opened in Douglas in 1891, Castle Rushen opened to tourists at a charge of 6d for adults and 2d for children. Pictured is William McLoughlin, the custodian of the castle for its first twenty-one years as a tourist attraction.

A temporary museum was set up in the banqueting hall of the castle in 1905. Among the exhibits was the skeleton of the giant Irish Elk which had been excavated at a site near St Johns and is still on display in the Douglas museum.

The Isle of Man Harriers met bi-weekly at locations all over the Island and their hounds were carried free of charge on the railway. The hunt was known to have met as often as 58 times in a season; the hounds being kennelled on the Old Castletown Road. Refreshments at the Castletown meet were usually provided at Balladoole.

The pillar in front of the castle glacis here is topped by an unusual thirteen faced lunar sundial which is supposed to be able to tell the time in various parts of the world by sun and moon. Dating from 1720, it was originally mounted on top of the former market cross.

Now housing offices, St Mary's church was the third church to be built on the site at the Market Place and until 1907 the Island's bishops were installed there. The octagonal lantern tower had to be taken down in 1912 for safety reasons.

The fifty foot pillar was erected to the memory of Governor Cornelius Smelt. He died at Castle Rushen in 1832 and was buried under the altar of St Mary's in three coffins of fir, lead and oak. However, he was clearly not as popular as had been thought as there was insufficient money to complete the memorial, let alone the statue on top proposed by Sir William Hillary. The Gawnes of Kentraugh paid the balance.

The shop at the junction of Malew and Arbory Street had until recently been a grocers for over a century, sixty years of which under the ownership of the Corlett family. In this 1923 view it still belonged to Jimmy Thomson who sold it to George and Fred Collister. George was well-known as captain of the town's football team.

Arbory Street contained several old established businesses including a joinery, saddlers, linen drapers and grocers. It was also a centre of the smuggling trade and several houses had vaults underground for storing contraband liquor. The Union Hotel on the left was visited by the writer George Borrow (author of *Romany Rye* and *Lavengro*) on his tour of the Island in 1855.

The windmill on Arbory Road was built in 1828 and throughout its life suffered damage to the sails from gale force winds – the reason why windmills are not common on the Isle of Man. There was also a fire in 1848 that reduced the building to ruins and although it was rebuilt and became a listed building, it is today an empty shell once more.

In the 1950s the building became famous as the Witches Mill when Dr Gerald Gardner converted the limestone barn by the mill into a restaurant and museum of witchcraft and magic. A Manx witch is traditionally an elderly woman who affects her neighbours directly, or indirectly through their possessions, by means of spells and charms. Dr Gardner only practised white magic but was constantly given requests for spells and love portions.

Lorne House was built on land belonging to Rushen Abbey in the late eighteenth century and extended in 1828. In 1834 it was occupied by the Lieutenant Governor, Colonel John Ready, continuing as Government House until the arrival of Governor Pigott in 1861. Now offices, most postcards of Lorne House date from the period 1931-1972 when it was a Christian Endeavour Holiday Home.

The first houses on the Crofts were built around 1830, but the history of the lands goes back to the 1640s when they were acquired by the Stanley family who ruled the Island between 1406 and 1736. The grounds formed part of the Lord of Mann's garden, and later the Governor's, before being acquired by the local architect Thomas Brine in the 1830s. The larger houses on the site include Westwood, Bagnio House and Crofton, once the home of local author Dr J. Clague.

Before 1874 the only entrance to the town for vehicles was from Douglas Street, via Bowling Green Road and Janet's Corner. The name was taken from the bowling green of the Lord of Mann and when prominent families started to build substantial homes in the capital, one of them was called Bowling Green House.

Rope making was an important craft in the Isle of Man and one of the oldest ropewalks on the Island, about 630 feet long, extended from Douglas Street to the west end of the promenade, running parallel to College Green.

Victoria Road was built about 1874, providing a more direct route into the town at the same time as the railway was reaching Castletown. Before this the path was so narrow that there was barely room for a cart to travel between the brewery and the river.

The verandah at Castletown Station has recently been removed as part of a scheme to return the building back to its original appearance. Supported on pillars, the verandah had been added in 1902 at a cost of £134.

The Silverburn was probably the most important source of water power on the Island and many mills have lined its banks over the centuries. The main period of mill construction was the eighteenth century and the Meadow Mill was typical of the period with its walls of local limestone and a roof of imported slate. The corn mill has been extensively restored although the wheel is no longer working.

The property on the Promenade was not developed for the tourist trade. Indeed, the main boarding house development (far right) was mostly bought up by King William's College after the First World War. Eight out of the eleven houses were used to accommodate the rapidly growing number of college boys, along with some huts from the staff quarters at Knockaloe Internment Camp.

King William's lost 127 old pupils and masters in the First World War. Their memorial cross was unveiled outside the college chapel in 1922.

The writer of this postcard says 'this is the junior house at King William's where Jack boards'. The house was photographed in 1905 by G.B. Cowen and is an unusual location to find a Ramsey photographer at work.

Engineering classes at the college started in 1892 and in 1904 the gymnasium was demolished and replaced by a new building concentrating on practical subjects. The ground floor included carpentry, metalworking and engineering shops which attempted to recreate real work conditions.

RONALDSWAY AERODROME, I.O.M.

During 1937 Ronaldsway was used by rival companies West Coast Air Services and Manx Airways Railway Air Services'. Passengers were insufficient to support both companies and a merger was quickly negotiated which resulted in Isle of Man Air Services Ltd.

Skillfully superimposed over this shot of Ronaldsway is a West Coast's Dragon G-ADCR. This was one of three added to their fleet in 1935, the year they were awarded a Post Office contract for mail between Liverpool and the Island. The limited facilities at the aerodrome can be seen left of centre; to the right is Ronaldsway Farm.

AERIAL VIEW OF RONALDSWAY. I.O.M.

G-ADCR

E.4281.

In 1933 the Edinburgh company British Flying Boats Ltd set up a service offering pleasure flights from Douglas and charter trips to the mainland. They used a Saro Cloud amphibian aircraft, *Cloud of Iona*, seen here over Port Erin. Using Ronaldsway as a base, the plane was a regular visitor to the South.

The Castletown Golf Links Hotel advertised itself as having the only natural links on the Island. There were also ample facilities for boating, bathing, fishing and a dancing pavilion if the guests tired with the golf. The hotel housed a gunnery school during the last war.

The Vikings found Ronaldsway a safe harbour and it was they who gave the name to the neck of land between Derbyhaven and Castletown bays. It is recorded that in 1226 when a southern gale was approaching, Olaf II of Mann dragged his five ships on rollers over Ronald's Way to Derbyhaven so that they could be launched safely.

Derbyhaven at the turn of the century.

The Derbyhaven Hotel enjoyed varying fortunes over the years but was particularly popular during the formative years of the nearby Ronaldsway Airport in the 1930s. The Marine Hydro Hotel, as it was still styled here, offered an attractive alternative to the primitive facilities on offer at the aerodrome.

The sensation of May 1925 was the beaching of the forty-eight foot Rudolph's Rorqual or Sei whale at Horse Gullet, Langness. It is thought that the whale had been struck by the liner Montrose of Queenstown a few days earlier and it was discovered by boys from King William's College. Its body was towed to Derbyhaven beach.

Overleaf: The whale's 3.5 ton skeleton is still on display in the Manx Museum. The transportation of the carcass to East Baldwin for treatment was a major operation involving two traction engines from Sulby Farm at Onchan. Despite the strong smell, the convoy drew large crowds. The carcass was then cleaned and prepared but it was not until ten years later that it was put on display in the museum's new natural history gallery.

Derbyhaven entertained other unexpected visitors. As the sender of this 1913 postcard explains, 'this is the ship that is wrecked on the golf links just under the college'.

The *Anna* left Maryport in April 1931, bound for her home port of Castletown with a cargo of coal. During the night of the twenty-first she ran aground near the old copper mines between the Skerranes and Dreswick Point, Langness. The crew of four made land safely in the small boat, but the ketch was a total wreck.

Great Meadow in Malew has been occupied since the twelfth century. The property has belonged to the Moore family for at least 300 years and the eighteenth century house presently standing there had impressive castellated extensions added in the nineteenth century. During the last war it served as an R.A.F. Officers' mess and is currently a horse stud with a particularly fine sham half timbered stable block.

Kirk Malew church dates from the thirteenth century. William Christian (Illiam Dhone) was buried in the chancel following his execution and the font is dedicated to his memory. It is said that some of the plotting of the revolt actually took place in the church, with the complicity of the vicar.

As a result of the Isle of Man (now Royal Manx) Agricultural Society's consistent failure to hold shows south of Douglas, the Southern District Agricultural Society started organising shows of its own in 1914. The first show, held that year, was a small affair but after 1920 they quickly developed and still attract large crowds.

An atmospheric view of the 'street' at Cross Four Ways, taken in 1903. The Smithy here was run by Jimmy Teare and all the old characters from the area would gather to exchange the skeet.

Ballasalla Post Office, *c.*1930, the scene of an unsolved murder in 1886. Having left for Castletown as usual, the mail cart was found without its driver, John Kermode. Thomas Tyson, the Ballasalla Postmaster and local policeman set up a search party and Kermode's body was soon found lying in a stream. There had been trouble over the tendering of the mail contract but nobody was ever charged with the crime.

The Methodist Church in Ballasalla has long been demolished and replaced by cottages but the nearest terrace on the right, Wesley Row, still survives.

These two views of Ballasalla at the turn of the century show the stark contrast with traffic conditions of today.

The Isle of Man first saw motor car racing in 1904 when trials were held to choose the British representative for the Gordon Bennett Cup competition which was to be held in France. Special laws had to be passed by the Manx parliament in order to close the appropriate roads. Initially the course covered the south of the Island but it was excluded after 1905.

The excitement at the Ballasalla control in 1904. The sender of this postcard proudly proclaimed that she had managed to 'get one of Clifford Earp'. Earp was very much the heartthrob of the young ladies of Mann. He had to wait another year, however, before representing his country in his Napier – he had a serious crash when taking part in the time trials on Douglas Promenade.

The Ballasalla control, which ended over a mile and a half away in Castletown, was one of five areas in which there was a speed limit to increase safety. The competitors were allowed over four minutes to cover this section. John Hargreaves is pictured here in his Napier at the Castletown end of the control. As in 1904 he was chosen as the reserve driver for the Gordon Bennett competition.

For a few brief years Ballasalla was home to the Island's Youth Hostel Association until different premises were opened at Bradda, Port Erin. Alas, there are no longer any youth hostels on the Island.

A very popular visiting place between the wars was Shimmin's Tea Gardens where the roundabout was a particular favourite with the children.

The ruins at Rushen Abbey are those of a Cistercian Monastery founded by Olaf I in 1134. It was dissolved in 1537 and the buildings were stripped of all materials of value, including the lead from the roofs and glass from the windows.

The Abbey's ruins were continually robbed of stones for the construction of buildings in the nearby village. The Abbey Hotel was no exception when it was built as a country house for Deemster Thomas Moore about 1765. It later became a girls school and has been run as a hotel since 1846.

In 1896 the Rushen Abbey Hotel and pleasure grounds were acquired by Thomas Cubbon of Douglas. Here, he and his son established a fruit growing estate and also expanded the summer restaurant with its speciality of strawberry and cream teas.

As well as the jam factory, a souvenir shop and facilities for dancing and afternoon and evening entertainment were added. As many as 4,000 would pay their 4d entrance money on a busy summer day and the tea dances were particularly popular.

The monks had two mills on the Silverburn and the whole area is full of reminders of their influence. The Abbot's or Abbey walk was accessible by a plank bridge and is still a tranquil riverside path today.

The Crossag or Monk's Bridge, 400 yards upstream from the Abbey, is the oldest on the Island and dates from about 1350. Only four feet wide, it is perhaps the best preserved packhorse bridge in Britain.

The wishing well on the Silverburn. Wells have played an important part in Manx folklore, particularly those that were supposed to be medicinal or curative. Typically the 'patient' would walk around the well in a sunwise direction, drink from the water, attach a fragment of clothing to a nearby tree or bush and drop in a pin, pebble or button.

Silverdale possesses a unique Victorian roundabout which was redesigned in 1911 to be water powered by a top fed wheel once used on the washing floor of the Foxdale mines. The carousel horses on the roundabout have been replaced by replicas, but some of the originals in this picture can be seen in the Silverdale cafe.

Known as the 'Chapel in the Mountains', St Marks' church was built in 1772 and provided only with a clay floor and earthen pews. The parsonage was swarming with rats and frequently awash with rain water, and chaplains rapidly came and went until things improved after 1827 under the Rev. J.T. Clarke who stayed for thirty years. Church Cottage, next to the church was originally divided into three alms houses which generated income to keep the school in repair.

The Moore family outside Santon Post Office. Three generations of the family ran the office from 1881 until Catherine Bridson took over in 1951.

St Sanctain's Church, Santon, stands on the site of an ancient keeill (or church) and the present building dates from 1774. A seventh century stone inscribed in Latin was found in the foundations and is claimed to be the only Roman monument on the Island. A disreputable past is rumoured with the possibility of a network of smugglers passages leading to the church and the fact that an early incumbent kept an ale house in the vicarage.

The tea gardens at Santon, *c*.1930.

Port Grenaugh was formerly the site of a large country farmhouse called Harbour House. It was demolished early this century and replaced by a shop, restaurant and fourteen self catering chalets. Today, only the gate pillars and boundary wall survive from the old house and even less of the tourist development.

The wreck of the steamer *Argo*, December 1905. On passage from Bordeaux to Glasgow with a general cargo, she struck rocks at Meary Voar near Santon Head. The crew of fourteen escaped safely at daybreak after a night spent trapped on the vessel. Continually pounded by the heavy seas, the wreck soon broke into three pieces.

Ballabeg straggles for some distance along the main Port Erin to Douglas road. Guidebook writers had little to say about its attractions except for the old barn at the Friary Farm which was formerly the chapel of an ancient Franciscan Friary.

The Essolene sign reflects changing times in this 1930s view of the smithy at Ballabeg.

The mill pond at Colby has recently been drained and unfortunately the thatched cottage on the right is also no more. The pond belonged to Cubbon's Mill, the only corn mill in the parish of Arbory.

The Colby river was vital to the village and the surrounding farms. There were five mills along its length – two at Kentraugh, the Little Mill, the Colby corn mill and the flax mill at the Scaard near the source of the river.

Colby, I.O.M.

Colby was popular with visitors seeking a more sedate holiday away from the large hotels and the bustle of the towns. Even in 1916 the writer of this card was surprised to find more visitors than he expected, but 'one could not find a better place than Colby to spend a short holiday'.

Running a sub post office has always involved working long hours; at the turn of the century the branch at Colby was open from 8 a.m. to 9 p.m.

The Colby Glen Hotel was popular with the horse drawn vehicles, or 'Kelly cars', that visitors used to tour the Island. The hotel's hostler was Jack Fielding who had been severely injured in a mine disaster and despite the loss of an arm and fingers had also been a tramp, scrap dealer and herring carter.

Quill's Cottage on the Main Road was popular with artists and photographers. Sadly now replaced by a modern house, the cottage was next to Elm Villa, home of Archibald Cregeen, compiler of the first Manx dictionary. The horse appears on several postcards and was obviously a valued member of the Quill family.

Miss Quayle's thatched cottage, known as 'California' was situated in an orchard on the Colby Glen Road. She ran this as a tea garden and it was popular with visitors who had walked up from the railway station.

Colby Station tended to be used by the locals only for special journeys such as monthly shopping trips to Douglas. This is the original 1874 building but it has been replaced by the small hut formerly sited at Kirk Braddan halt.

The Youth Hostel at the Level, Colby, was the first on the Island and opened in 1937. The hostel stood by the current bus stop at the Level, having been demolished as part of a road widening scheme.

Croit-e-Caley farm was formerly owned by the Kneen family, who having seen John Wesley preach locally, were responsible for the spread of Methodism in the area. Services were originally held in a building loaned by the owner of Kentraugh Mill until the Primitive Methodist Ebenezer Chapel was built in 1881. The area is now home to a popular fruit farm.

The unusual outbuildings at Kentraugh farm, including the louvred cupola, have featured on many paintings over the years. The house and lodge date from the 1830s and were possibly designed by the famous architect John Welch.

These cottages at Kentraugh were occupied by mill employees until production stopped in 1943. The mill dates possibly from as early as 1500 but is now without its wheel and dam.

The mill referred to in the caption is Rhenwyllin Mill which shared its water supply with a nearby smelting works, hence 'the Smelt'. In the mid-nineteenth century lead ore was transported here from the Bradda Head and Ballacorkish mines.

Roland and Fred Bates's Shore Hotel was quietly situated on the shore away from the town. The owners stressed the select nature of the clientele and the hotel boasted a garage at a time when few holiday makers could have afforded a car.

This view of Sea Crest (the large block in the centre) on the Shore Road at Brewery Beach has undergone considerable change over the years. The buildings on the left have been replaced by modern housing and a sea wall has been constructed which, even with the addition of thousands of tons of rocks, has not always provided adequate protection against the encroaching waves.

The name Gansey relates to just a small area around Gansey Point and doesn't extend to the nearby mill at the Smelt and certainly not the whole bay. The area in this picture is more built up today but is still one of the prettiest bays on the Island.

Originally the station at Port St Mary had been a mere wooden shelter and in 1891 local residents had campaigned for 'increased accommodation' which would be of a style more in keeping with the middle and upper class holiday makers attracted to the area. The extensive red brick building (far left), which except for Douglas is the Island's largest station house, was eventually built in 1898 along with a platform, good sheds, cattle dock and hotel.

Next door to the new station was the equally impressive Station Hotel. Run by Mrs Timperley from Manchester, terms were 6/6d per day when this postcard was produced in 1906.

Four Roads marked the boundary between Port Erin and Port St Mary and was the site of occasional disturbances between the youths of the two areas. The runic monument, here just out of picture, is the largest on the Island. Four Roads no longer contains any shops but it was once home to Ned's Blacksmiths and Mammy Dibb's sweet shop, beloved of generations of local children.

The old tennis courts were once on the site of the Coronation boating pool although they were relocated in 1936 to a spot by the station at Four Roads, shown here.

For the Manx residents the old town by the harbour remained the centre of Purt-le-Murray although with the development of tourism and the arrival of new residents the newer parts flourished. This 1930s view of Bay View Road shows R.K. Kermode the chemists; other shops included Maggie Gawne's, Collister's 'Rest-a-While Cafe', and Watterson's gentlemen's outfitters – later Smokey Joe's Cafe.

Station Road, 1909. Among the shops here is W.H. Gill's general store. His specialities were Danish butter, Irish bacon and fresh ground coffee.

The Cliff Hotel on the right (later the Golf Links Hotel) was built in 1886. Until then the only accommodation had been at the Bay Hotel and Ship Hotel but the Cliff still only brought the tourist capacity of the whole village up to about one hundred.

The hotel is still open as a public bar but the accommodation is now residential and the building is known as the Carrick Flats. The view from the back shows the very distinctive style of construction, built sheer down to the water.

In the 1920s the post office was situated on Bay View Road next to the Bay View Hotel. For many years the postmaster was H.B. Jones who published numerous postcards of Port St Mary.

In 1887 part of the Ballacreggan Estate was divided into building plots which were later sold to form the basis of the promenade.

The place to hire a bathing hut was near the slipway on the lower promenade. The huts had a carrying handle on each corner of the base and could be moved easily along the beach or even onto the slipway itself when the tide was high.

Founded by Robert Matheson (Mr Matt) the Childrens' Special Service Mission has been run every August since 1901 from Dublin House on the promenade. The fortnight of services, beach games and competitions would end with a candlelight procession and party featuring a big cake such as this one.

Ballaqueeney, as the Bay Queen Hotel was formally known, grew from these humble beginnings to become famous throughout the north of England. The buildings had various extensions, the latest and largest of which took place in 1935. By then the hotel could accommodate three hundred guests and had a hundred staff who worked an unusually long twenty week season.

Harold Moorhouse's band played at the hotel for 39 years and their Sunday evening concerts were very popular and raised a lot of money for charity. Celebrities such as Kathleen Ferrier the opera singer and Violet Carson of Coronation Street fame gave their services free of charge.

Some of the smaller cottages in Port St Mary were built of shore stone, usually gathered by horse and cart from the area south of the Point Hotel. This is one of the fishermen's cottages on the Underway which runs along the shore line by the harbour.

Maggie 'the Brew' Cregeen (does anyone know why she had this nickname?), outside her cottage with her son Tom who is sitting by the boy with the milk can. He was a fisherman who also carried the visitors luggage from the station to the hotel. He was nicknamed 'Sullivan' as he had once been tipped a sovereign and never having seen one before mistakenly called it a sullivan.

Fishing boats at Port St Mary.

Around eighty Manxmen were employed in Port St Mary for the cleaning, gutting, salting, curing and barrelling of the herring catch and they were helped by a large number of Scottish and Irish girls. The quantity of barrels visible behind the lifeboat house gives an indication of the size of the operation. The start of each season was marked by the arrival of boats from the Baltic stacked high with the empty barrels.

FILLING UP HERRING PORT ST MARY

The export trade was largely with Germany, Russia and the Low Countries. A team of three women, two gutters and one packer, could clean about one thousand herring in an hour – enough for only three barrels. Crowds of onlookers would gather and sometimes bets would be laid on two teams set to work against each other.

Gutter girls wore oilskin aprons and wellington boots. They also bandaged their hands to protect their fingers from a slip of the knives, but their skill was such that accidents were rare.

When the fish buyers and suppliers arrived to bargain with the fishermen at the quayside market the narrow streets of the port became very busy. Most of the catch was for export and carts such as this one unloaded the catch into large troughs for the attention of the gutter girls.

Herring were counted into a basket in threes or 'warps', 40 of which, along with an extra warp and one extra herring, made up a 'long hundred' of 124 fish. Five 'long hundreds' made a 'mease' of 620 herring. More recently fish have been counted by placing them in 'quarter cran' baskets – a cran contains around two or three mease, depending on the size of the fish.

The *Mary Jane* was built in 1879 and gave thirty-five years of service before being broken up in 1915. In 1890 the fleet contained 104 boats but by 1910 it had shrunk to forty-three. By 1930 only two of the old boats survived as most of the fishing fleet had been replaced by new motor vessels.

The *Mary Jane* is visible again here in the centre of the row to the left. All the Port St Mary fleet were registered at Castletown.

The *Elate* (CT22) was built in 1876 but soon after this photogrpah was taken she was wrecked after running aground near the Alfred Pier in 1908. The lifeboat saved the fifteen people on board, including the famous local artist William Hoggatt.

As well as the large fleet of nobbies and nickeys (Manx names for the types of fishing boats), the tall masts and rigging of schooners could also be seen in the harbour. They were manned by local crews and names such as the *Venus*, the *Jilt* and the *Gold Seeker* were well known. They were involved in the coastal and ocean going trade, usually carrying general cargoes.

Motor power started to make an impact on the fishing fleet in the 1890s and soon the only sail carried by the Nobbies was a small one aft to keep the head of the vessel to the wind. Some skippers are said to have taken the magneto home every morning to keep it in the oven to guard against dampness.

The Alfred Pier was named after the then Duke of Edinburgh who laid the foundation stone in January 1882. Built of limestone, the pier was completed five years later and much improved the shelter available to the fishing fleet.

Progress in the industry continued and by the 1920s steam drifters such as the *Rock Daisy* were replacing the motor nobbies. They were quicker and more efficient, arriving home first with the catch and getting the best prices. Boats from Yarmouth and Lowestoft joined the Scottish drifters during the interwar period and it is significant that none of the drifters in this postcard are Manx registered.

The inner harbour at Port St Mary was known as Port Vark and the Watch House and wall of Albert Hotel at the bottom of the harbour were popular places for fishermen to meet and share the skeet.

Lime Street takes its name from the two large lime kilns formerly used to burn the stone near the site of the present breakwater. Before the installation of water mains the nearest well for residents of the street was where the yachting pool is now situated. Water would be in short supply in late summer and some people would fetch their water as early as 4 a.m.

Established in 1896, the lifeboat station at Port St Mary was the last to be opened on the Island. This is the first lifeboat and crew outside the new boathouse – the *James Stevens* saved thirty-nine lives between 1896 and 1917.

The first motor lifeboat at Port St Mary, the *Sir Heath Harrison*, arrived in 1936. It served until 1948 and saved thirty-one lives. Each year on the morning of Lifeboat Day the boat was slowly pulled up the Port to the Bayqueen and money was collected in a canvas sheet.

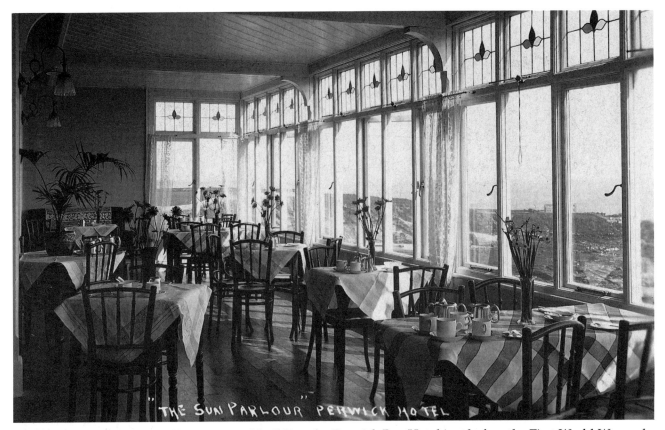

The local hotelier, Thomas Clague, started building the Perwick Bay Hotel just before the First World War and it was completed by his son in 1916. On opening the price for accommodation was 8/6d a day.

By 1936 it was advertised as the Perwick Bay and Links Hotel as it adjoined the new golf course. Other facilities included the private beach and 100 foot swimming pool. The wealthier guests were met by hotel cars at the Ronaldsway airstrip.

Perwick beach before the development of the swimming pool. On the beach there is a small cave said to have been used by smugglers and connected by a passage to another cave on the Cat Walk.

On the road to the Chasms lies Fistard. It was still relatively isolated at the turn of the century and the wearing of traditional Manx costume by the older inhabitants would not have just been for the benefit of the photographer. Although near to Port St Mary the only day to day contact the hamlet normally had with the outside world was with the local tradesmen who visited the outlying communities selling produce from their carts.

Glenn Chass was a favourite spot of Manx poet T.E. Brown and the line in his poem *Clifton*, 'And gorse runs riot in Glen Chass – thank God' is one of his most famous. As early as 1700 the area was mined for copper and two stone chimneys belonging to the mine buildings still remain today.

As there was once no road below Glen Chass corner, the road to the Howe was important from an early date as it formed part of the route between Cregneash and Port St Mary. The Howe was the original preaching place of the Island's first Wesleyans.

The Howe Road was far too narrow to take the tourist charabancs, restricting the number of visitors who could reach the Sound and Cregneash. Road widening was eventually carried out in the 1930s as one of the Manx Highway Board's public works schemes which were operated in the days before unemployment benefit.

Cregneash, c.1900, looking down the Chasms Road toward Harry Kelly's cottage, the first building on the left of the road. Some of the two storey houses in the village today, such as the weavers house, were still single storey traditional cottages at this time.

Church services at Cregneash had been held in one of the farmhouses until St Peters church was finally opened in 1878. This simple building cost very little to build as the work was carried out for free by the local people. The church also initially doubled as a school.

The Karran farm is the last traditional Manx crofting farmstead on the Island and originally it covered about thirty acres. As well as farming the Karran family, whose members were noted for their giant stature, were also involved in fishing and quarried slate from the cliff face at Spanish Head.

The best known building in Cregneash is this early eighteenth century cottage, last occupied by Harry Kelly, crofter and fluent Manx speaker, whose family lived in the village for over three hundred years. The lady facing the camera is his mother.

Bradda Head from the Darrag. Prior to the introduction of the binder machine, corn was cut by a horse drawn reaper and during the harvest all the local people would be involved in some way. Children followed the reaper knotting bands of corn straw, while the women lifted the corn and placed it on a band so that a man following behind could tie it into a sheaf. At the end of this procession would be the 'stookers' who placing five sheaves on either side to form stooks to be left to dry in the sun.

The Clan Line steamer, *Clan MacMaster*, hit the Thousla rock in dense fog in September 1923. Luckily she sank very slowly so that the crew were able to get off safely and much of her cargo (including sewing machines) was salvaged. It is said that some of the saved sewing machines are still in use in the south of the Island today.

The Calf of Man, near Port Erin, I.O.M.

South Harbour is the principal landing place on the Calf of Man but there are also small concrete landing stages at Grant's Harbour, above, and Carey's Harbour. Just beyond the store house on the left is Cow Harbour, so called as the cattle would be swum across to here from the mainland. This was done at slack water and the beasts were fastened by their horns to a rowing boat and guided across.

The waters around the Calf of Man are very treacherous and particular hazards include Chicken Rock which lies a mile offshore. Two lighthouses were built on the Calf in 1818 but proving ineffective, public pressure led to a new one being erected on the Rock in 1875. Nevertheless, a number of vessels have come to grief in the area over the years, including the *S.S. Irrawaddy* which ran onto the rocks below the two disused lighthouses in 1905.

Another ship in distress to draw a crowd and one which proved that it wasn't only the waters round the Calf that were treacherous was the *Mona's Isle III*. She was the first of five paddle steamers added to the Manx fleet during the 1880s and the largest and most expensive in the fleet at the time. Returning from Dublin in September 1892 she went aground at Scarlett Point with 400 passengers on board. After being stuck for two days she was successfully refloated with the help of the steamship *Tynwald*, seen here in the background.

Work to rebuild Port Erin station began in 1902 and took three years due to a dispute with the Commissioners who insisted that the new building should stand further from the road. During 1903 a temporary building had been necessary while the Ruabon brick building was completed.

After the station was finally finished it still proved inadequate for traffic at the busiest times and in 1911 the platform had to be extended and additional sidings constructed.

Athol Park is the only public park in Port Erin and although small it is charmingly laid out around the sheltered stream and former Athol Wood. Most of the properties skirting the park were developed for tourist accommodation.

Station Road, *c.*1920. Shops in this stretch included R.H. Kennaugh's Central Stores, Taylor's Bazaar, Duggan's Confectioners and T.H. Thomas's Tobacconist and Hairdressers. Every morning Thomas's would send an assistant to the hotels and boarding houses to shave guests if required.

The Falcon's Nest, opened in 1860, is the oldest hotel in Port Erin. Every comfort and luxury was offered by the 32 room hotel, including sea bathing, fishing, stabling for fifty horses and 'splendid rifle practice for Volunteers, at any range amongst the rocks'!

This early view looking across Falcon Hill shows the various thatched cottages which would soon be demolished in the redevelopment of the area.

Down by the pier, Port Erin still gave every impression of being a working harbour, even if so much of the boatman's livelihood now depended on following the tourist rather than the herring.

The redeveloped property on Falcon Hill, or Strand Road. J.J. Kneen had another shop on Breakwater Road but this Falcon Hill branch was a newsagents with a circulating library. Postcards were a speciality and visitors were recommended to try his toffee and Port Erin rock – the only rock made in the district.

Over two hundred rowing boats and fifty licensed boatmen were available for hire in Port Erin's sheltered bay. Reliable boats cost 1/9d per hour with the services of the boatman or 1/- without.

A young holidaymaker engages the boatman in conversation, although it was usually the visiting anglers who sought their attention. By getting on the right side of the boatman many useful hints could be obtained regarding the best fishing grounds and the most suitable tackle and bait.

An Edwardian family, somewhat overdressed for the beach, negotiate the hire of a suitable vessel.

Many were just as happy to sample the delights of sea and sand.

Boats were often hired by bathing parties to reach the smaller coves but note the bathing platform in the bay on the right. As an alternative to the baths tourists could swim from here for a charge of 6d, fortified by a 2d 'half rum and milk'. It would appear that extra care would be needed to avoid the traffic but at least the lifeboat is present on this occasion.

The outer breakwater had its foundations destroyed in a storm in 1884 and it was not until 1913 that work commenced on a new inner breakwater to provide shelter for the fishing and pleasure boats. This included the building of the new Raglan pier, bottom left.

The Port Erin lifeboat station opened in 1883 and the boat house (now a public shelter) was completed the following year. The special launching carriage shown here enabled the boat to be easily dragged to the harbour or hauled to Fleshwick or even Port St Mary depending on conditions.

Port Erin lifeboat's first coxswain was W. Collister who served until 1898 and was succeeded by Joseph Woodworth.

CREW OF THE LIFEBOAT
"ETHEL DAY CARDWELL"
PORT ERIN,
I.O.M.

The port's first motor lifeboat, introduced in 1925, was the *Ethel Day Cardwell* and she is seen here being launched down the new slipway – the steepest of any station in Britain and still in use today. The *Ethel Day Cardwell* remained on station until 1939 and saved four lives during nineteen service launches.

The Port Erin Marine Biological Station opened in the old mortuary buildings below the Belle Vue Hotel in 1892 before moving to its present site, above, in 1902. The laboratory became part of Liverpool University in 1919 although its fish hatchery remained under the control of the Manx government.

The small museum and public aquarium at the Station was opened in 1902 and is shown here prior to modernisation in 1954. A clause had been placed in the agreement with Liverpool University to ensure continued public access and 43,000 people visited in 1938.

The building facing on the left is the George Herdman Institute (The Toot) which once housed the town library. It was converted from shops by Professor Herdman, director of the Marine Biological Station, and named in memory of his son who was killed on the Somme. The ground floor was a recreation room for the fishermen and boatmen with a library above. No alcohol or gambling was allowed.

S.S. Sabina beached in Port Erin Bay. Yet another victim of the rocks around the Calf of Man, she was brought into the bay to undergo repairs.

Another attraction in Port Erin, this cafe was famed for its fish and chips.

Much of the residential development along Bay View Road dates from the interwar period, but as early as 1903 the first holiday accommodation was being advertised. Avondale, Ivydene and Lonsdale were all boarding houses on the road and each had seven bedrooms available.

Dandy Hill typifies the older parts of Port Erin that helped to make the village so popular with the visitors. The ancient road from Cregneash follows a route via Balnahowe and Dandy Hill and leads down to the old village situated by the beach.

St Mary's Road, 1930s. At that time the attractions here were the Breadle Glen Tennis Courts and the adjoining pitch and putt course. Weekly knockout tennis tournaments were held during the season along with competitions between guests of rival hotels.

Shore Road before the construction of the promenade wall. As they were constructed piecemeal between 1879 and 1894 the hotels have a pleasing variety of architectural styles.

The local authority was closely involved in the running of the beach and facilities were excellent. Uniformed attendants were in charge of the large numbers of deck chairs and bathing machines. The beach tents could be rented by the day, week or month from the grandly titled Deck Chair Superintendent.

The Cosy Nook Cafe was part of the oldest section of the village. The old St Catherine's well and pump stood between Shore View Garden and St Catherine's Terrace Gardens down at beach level. Before the days of piped water, the water jugs on hotel tables were filled from here.

After the marine laboratory moved in 1902, the old building down on the shore became St Columba's Catholic Chapel. This was mainly for the benefit of Catholic holidaymakers and closed during the winter. The two local Catholic families then had to travel to Castletown.

Maypoles are an ancient fertility symbol but the be-ribboned short poles and ribbon dances below were only introduced to the Island by English residents in the nineteenth century.

Collinson's Cafe was a favourite feature of Port Erin for over half a century. Situated in Spaldrick bungalow on the cliff side, the grounds extended right down to the beach and the views from the cafe were some of the finest on the Island. The spectacular semi-circular ballroom was added in the 1920s and an orchestra played there daily.

The cafe and the adjoining shops. The Greensill's Mona Bouquet was a local perfume first produced in 1852.

The Traie Meanagh Baths were advertised as the largest sea water baths in the British Isles. An engine supplying 520 gallons of sea water per minute ensured 'fresh' water daily until closure in 1981. The diving boards and water shutes were popular and galas were held weekly throughout the season.

Bathing was mixed from the start and the ladies dressing rooms and the refreshment facilities are shown here. Viewing accommodation was limited within the baths but there was space for hundreds of spectators on benches in terraces on the cliff side.

THE HUT CAFE AND GROUNDS, PORT ERIN, I.O.M.

Bradda Glen cafe, known as 'the Hut', was built during the mid-nineteenth century as a holiday home by the owner of the Bellevue Zoo in Manchester. The thatched building was used as a club house before being taken over as a cafe and ballroom in 1920. 'The hut' expanded to become Collinson's holiday camp, a reconstruction made possible with the help of huts and materials from the Knockaloe Internment Camp.

The view from the top of the promenade towards Bradda reveals the mini building boom of the 1920s.

The Port Erin Golf Club was opened as a nine hole course in 1895 and extended to full size by 1910. Few locals could afford to play at the time and the club's fortunes depended on the growing holiday trade.

The proprietors of the Bay Cliff Hotel were for many years Mr and Mrs Moore who offered special terms to golfers. The hotel boasted a recreation hall and this made it particularly suitable for conversion to a youth hostel in the 1950s.

Mining has taken place at Bradda since prehistoric times but most extensively in the years between 1850 and 1883, although the output of lead and copper was disappointing. Above is the 'eye' of Bradda and the office of the Bradda mine which still survives along with the engine house and smithy which are visible from Port Erin harbour.

The water supply to Port Erin was once supplied by two small reservoirs at Surby, a tiny hamlet lying one and a half miles north. The village was also the home for many years of a famous brass band which became the Rushen Silver Band.

Fleshwick was a Viking landing place and the battle site of a famous eleventh century Celtic victory. Crebbin's tea rooms on the brows above the shore offered tennis courts, camping and fresh farm produce.

Fleshwick was a popular destination for boating excursions, although boats could be hired there as well for fishing or exploring the nearby caves. Above is the tiny tea and ginger beer shop which was a feature on the beach for many years.

SOME FURTHER READING

The following books are among many that deal with the south of the Island. The out of print titles should be available in local libraries or through good second hand bookshops. Sadly, very little of the work of some fine local writers such as Cecil McFee seems to have been published in book form.

Anon. — *History of the Parish of Kirk Arbory and its Church of St Columba*, 1959

Brand, Andy and Hawkins, S. — *Dredging Up the Past*, 1992

Clague, Dr J. — *Manx Reminiscences*, 1911 (reprinted 1991)

Duffield, John — *Kirk Christ Rushen*, 1951

Kniveton, G.N. — *Rushen Abbey: a History and Guide*, 1988

Looney, A.M. (ed.) — *History of Laa Columb Killey 1912-1986*, 1986

Manx Museum — *A Guide to Cregneash*, 1985

Marshall, W. Lockington — *Calf of Man*, 1978

Morris, Jeff — *Story of Port Erin Lifeboats 1883-1983*, 1983

Quillam, John — *Know Your Parish* (3 vols), 1979-1981

Ralfe, P.G. — *Parish Church of St Mary, Castletown*, 1926

Reid, Alan — *Rowany Golf Club Centenary*, 1995

Rigby, Armitage — *Castle Rushen*, 1927

Rodgers, Kate — *A Circular Tour of Port St Mary*, 1980

Rodgers, Kate (ed.) — *Our Heritage* (4 vols.), 1986-1988

Stowell, Flaxney — *Castletown a Hundred Years Ago*, 1902

Watterson, Harry — *The Port St Mary Fishing Fleet of 1886*, 1986

The lighthouse at Langness, together with the three keepers' houses,
was built in 1880. It has since been automated.